POEMS OF LOVE AND WAR

ROBERT HILLIARD

Poems of Love and War © 2018 Robert Hilliard. All rights reserved. Big Table Publishing Company retains the right to reprint. Permission to reprint must be obtained from the author, who owns the copyright.

ISBN: 978-1-945917-25-7

Printed in the United States of America

Cover Art: Jo-Ann Hilliard

Also by Robert Hilliard:
Phillipa
The Greener Trees
Surviving the Americans
Hollywood Speaks Out
Media, Education, And America's Counter-Culture Revolution
*Waves Of Rancor**
*Dirty Discourse**
*The Broadcast Century And Beyond**
*The Hidden Screen**
*The Quieted Voice**

*Co-author with Michel C. Keith

"Making other books jealous since 2004"

Big Table Publishing Company
Boston, MA
www.bigtablepublishing.com

Acknowledgments

My thanks to my long-time co-author Michael Keith for putting me in touch with Big Table Publishing Company, where I have had the special pleasure of working with editor Robin Stratton, whose continuing and prompt attention to this, my first book of poems, felt like I was the publisher's special author. I appreciate poet Joe Pacheco's invitation to join his Sanibel Writer's Group to write poetry and the feedback from the members of the group at the first reading of many of these poems. As I write new poems for an intended second book of poetry, I continue to be grateful for the encouragement of, and poetry at night with, Jo-Ann, to whom this book is dedicated.

To Jo-Ann
Whose poetry at night made this volume possible.

It was reading poetry at night that prompted me to attempt to write poetry again. "Again" means after some 70 years of writing non-fiction and fiction books, newspaper and periodical articles, and plays. Before that, in the Army in World War II, and in college afterward, I wrote poetry, some of which is included in this collection.

Table of Contents

Poetry at Night	11
For Jo-Ann, Love Senses	12
Cuddling	14
The Song	16
Love is?	17
A Belly Bare	18
Mildady	19
A Dashing Lad Was He	20
Blind Love	22
The Mariner	23
Did I See Versailles…?	26
Black Blood	28
War is a Whore	33
A Soldier's Thoughts	34
An English Girl's WWII Lament	36
Wordsworth, Where Art Thou?	39
From My Bedroom Window	40
Tumbling	43
The Deer	44
Sleep	46
Save a Teardrop	48
O, America, November 8, 2016	49
Silence	53
There Came a Tyrant	54
RIP: A Sixty-Year Lament	56
Cyberspace	59
Marlowe on a Soccer Field	60
Fear	62
Life Span	63
Am I My Grandfather?	64
The Sun	65
Kitty Ditty	66
The Soul is not Betrayed	67
Were I to Climb Every Hill	68
Life Is	69
Dreams	70

POETRY AT NIGHT

I do enjoy poetry at night.
It pierces the darkness,
turns shadows into light.
My heart it does caress.

I do enjoy the verses
brimming o'er the book,
bringing bounty to my soul,
to every cranny and nook.

I do enjoy the symphonic sounds
no matter what the rhyme.
The words rush through my head
and pass too quick in time.

My eyes soon close,
no more is read,
but the poems still float
o'er my night-time bed.

While others stare at flickering screens
'tis books of poems that give me light.
What better manna for my senses
than reading poetry at night!

FOR JO-ANN. LOVE SENSES

We see a smiling face, we hear a lovely voice, but how often are all of our five senses—sight, sound, smell, taste, touch—stimulated by feelings of love?

What treasures do I see
through smokeless clouds
and pearls of dew?
A pleasure dome?
A spring of gold?
Or is my sight of you?

What pounding do I hear
in dark-stilled night?
From placid seas?
A tree that falls?
A mermaid's call?
Or my heart rapt in thee?

What words across my lips
come forth
as feelings inside grow?
No parables
or mundane speech
for love's literate glow.

What secrets do my fingers touch
and bring to life
beneath the sheath so fair?
Still untouched words
and newborn sighs
so far beyond compare!

What Cathay scents,
perfumes Paree,
aromas of distant lands
fill my soul with sweetness,
my heart with ecstasy?
Your presence near at hand.

What taste of honey
do I savor?
Cherry from your lips,
a gourmet feast
of requited love,
incomparable bliss!

CUDDLING
Someone once asked, on a cold winter's night, "do you want to keep warm with the fireplace or with bodies?" Fortunate are they who don't have to hesitate before answering.

I cannot sleep the night
without a cuddling by.
Neither music, words nor mystic light,
not even an earthy sigh
will rest my body
or my soul.
And touch that misses
wide the mark
leaves me spare
and cold.

Come back, thou,
with cuddling joy.
To savor the night
come full to me, reserveth not,
bring succor to my plight.
To sleep, to dream
in deep esteem
of Morpheus nightly plot.
But absent she who cuddles best,
it cannot be my lot.

Look high, look low
and hope to find
the answer to a sleepless night
and hold me in its bind.

No more to search,
no more to lurch,
no more my mind to muddle.
It takes two sets
of open arms
to spend the night in cuddle.

THE SONG

Experiencing war up close as a combat infantry soldier may push a teenager into abrupt adulthood, yet the inner child may remain dormant, resisting the reality of war. One part of the inner child is romantic shyness, nurtured by the neo-Victorian mores that dominated much of American society prior to World War II. As a returning college student, I wrote the following in 1947, a comment on the feeling and behavior of myself and other students.

Can silence reveal the echo
of the lonely heart?
Will mute refrain bring melody
from the melodious harp?

The strings are silent, but the hand
that plays knows well the part.

The fingers that pluck the chords
must grasp the tune.
Then would the gilded strings play,
the gentle notes divinely hewn.

Yet, should the strings be left untouched,
t'will not in tranquil silence bloom,
but wither and die,
the song untuned.

LOVE IS?

Some people believe that love is a totality of giving, which, if true, has the counterpart of a totality of taking. Even a once-popular romantic song said "take all of me." But isn't true love, in fact, not giving or taking, but sharing?

"Falling in love is wonderful,"
Berlin wrote, "so they say."
Staying in love
takes stronger will
not meant for feet of clay.

Do you give all to love
and keep nothing for yourself?
Or do you hoard the innermost
of who you are
hidden away on a secret shelf?

How much of me is given
for someone else to own?
Or is love, in truth,
a passing fancy
meant for just a loan?

How quick to love
do lovers leap
before they ask
what part of me
might I well keep!

A BELLY BARE

A belly bare
that is so fair
pillowed by my side.

Soft open lips
and flowing hips,
the better for to ride.

A well-turned breast
on which to rest,
the rise and fall of tide.

No lust is here
for one so dear
for love is all to bide.

A hand caress
does not access
beyond the velvet skin.

A being whole,
both sense and soul,
must reach the heart within.

MILADY

No need to light the lamp,
send the lamplighter on his way.
Her eyes aglow provide the beam
of stars that shine by day.

No need to lay the fire
that warms the evening's essence.
The night is fulsome filled
by Milady's very presence.

No need to try to reach one's heart
with mime or word or rhyme.
'Tis all apiece forever more,
Milady says she's mine!

A DASHING LAD WAS HE
Reading Robert Burns educes not only a feeling for place and time, but often a sense of irony. So many of Burns's poems are short stories in verse. I wrote the following, an irony of love, after an evening of reading Burns's poetry.

A dashing lad was he
who ne'er sought company
sans charm and wit and wherewithal
to bring him joys both large and small.

An everyman, that he was not.
He sought fame, fortune and privileged lot.

But alas for him the day doth come
when a lass he met became the sum
of stars and moon and sun so bright
his thoughts of her were day and night.

He hemmed and hawed, fussed and fumed,
the new-found love his libertine doomed.

This lass was neither high-born poor
nor low-born rich. Should he seek a dower?
For once, to him, it didn't matter.
Her charm his judgment put in tatters.

This lass, she was so bonnie fair,
despite himself, could he not care?

More and deeper than e'er before
his heart so quick was fulsome sore,
could not dismiss this lassie's lure,
knew soon enough that love was sure.

Lost in love ne'er known to him,
what went before now grey and dim.

He looked upon her heaving breast
and quickly put all doubts to rest.
Open arms he could not resist
from dusk to dawn was new-found bliss.

Ah, he who thought himself so smart
doth let his head give way to heart.

So fully did this lad succumb,
no more the piper or the rum,
for soon he reached another sum:
husband and father to become.

Where has it gone, the life he led?
Not totally gone, but in a new-made bed.

BLIND LOVE

The blind, they say, see many things
our sight conceals from view.
And love, they say, is blind, but dear,
can what they say be true?
For where I once saw many things
I now see only you.

THE MARINER
(Not So Ancient, He)

Oh me, oh my,
how she doth sigh,
No words come from her lips.
What thoughts escape the ruby door
'bout ocean's painted ships?

She moves her head,
so slight it treads.
recalling things of past,
a sailor on a wooden deck,
all that, that she holds fast.

A tale within
she would exhale
of mariners and earthly whales,
of marriage vows and honeymoons,
of sultry nights and bright-lit noons.

So why
within her sparkling eye
does sadness so regretful lie?
T'was not an Albatross to blame,
no crossbow put her thoughts to shame.

A mariner, a promised match,
a life less sober to unlatch.
At last, at last, the promised joy
for her, the girl,
for him, the boy.

Pleasures she had ever sought,
at last, at last—but danger fraught.
Hie, hie, to shore,
she'll not be late
to meet her promised handsome mate.

A mariner come from afar
like Apollo from a star
to make her dreams reality,
to take her back
with him to sea.

The mighty calm had come too soon,
pierc'ed by a waning moon.
The ship raced home a'front the storm.
Oh, please, she begged,
bring no harm.

Now winds blew heavy 'cross the sky,
the prow dipped low, then far too high.
Thunder, lightning ringed the ship.
She watched in horror,
bit her lip.

Come quickly, please,
do not delay,
I fear there'll be no other day.
Her pleas rose to an angry sky.
Too late, too late, she heard the cry.

Her mariner on deck stood tall,
then slowly he began to fall,
the ship crashed heavily
into the main,
her voice cried no, rapt in pain.

The night turned black, naught to see,
the ship sunk deep despite her plea.
No moon, no stars, an empty void.
An empty ocean,
no human motion.

She sits alone, with lonely sighs,
no words can match her silent cries.
Just thoughts of what
might have been hers
had she not lost her mariner.

DID I SEE VERSAILLES . . . ?

On May 7, 1945, World War II in Europe ended. I was a 19-year-old Purple Heart combat infantry veteran eager to return home to "The States." When I was finally discharged in early 1946, I found many well-meaning people back in America who did not have the slightest idea what our combat servicemen and women had experienced, and wrote this poem.

Did I see Versailles and the Eiffel Tower,
DeGaulle or Patton or Eisenhower?
Don't know as I did, sir, I spent my time
right up front on the firing line
where we saw only mud that reached our knees
and our skin would crack and our feet would freeze,
where there were no cities or generals,
just rubble and dirt and sickening smells.
There were no chateaus, no sights to pick.
I'm sorry, sir, just damned Krauts to lick.

Did I see the castles upon the Rhine
or the blue Danube that flowed like wine?
The only rivers that I saw there
were the rivers of blood while men would swear
and bind their wounds and wait for aid
and live . . . and wait for aid and die . . . afraid.
Our castles were deep, four feet or so
out of frozen earth and filled with snow
and rocks and dirt that the shells would flick.
We were busy, sir. Damned Krauts to lick.

Did I see the fields and small canals
and the snow-capped peaks of the tow'ring Alps?
Yes, I saw the fields with their many dead
and the fresh green grass that was now blood red,
and the streets and paths with their waiting mines

and the booby-traps at the German lines.
I looked on high for the Alps but found
only bloody pieces of men on the ground.

I saw them sir: hell and death so quick.
You see, sir, we had the damned Krauts to lick.

BLACK BLOOD

We entered World War II to fight for freedom and equality. Or so we were told. There are no "good" wars, but I believed then, and still do, that World War II was a necessary war, one to stop fascism and genocide from dominating even more of the world. But I did not see the same freedom being applied to all of us who thought we were fighting for it. I put my thoughts into the following piece while in combat in Europe in 1944.

It was quiet.
No more noise.
The shooting, roar of guns, awful pounding
gone.
Nothing remained but mud,
filthy wet mud
covering
face, hands, body.
Mud that oozed
from the soft ground
as blood from . . .
blood?
Blood all over and
hot, burning pain.
Blood that made you sick to your stomach,
pain that made you grit your teeth.

But now they were gone.
They wouldn't come again
to charge
like hideous monsters
bent on destruction.
Eyes gleaming, mouths snarling
they had come.
Ten, twenty, thirty
with guns
to kill.

Run!
Legs won't move.
Charge!
Cannot.
Wet, shivering, cold . . . warm.
Scared!
Raise your rifle.
They were only men
of flesh . . . and blood
and would die.
But
they had rifles, too,
that spurted flame
and noise
and . . .

Pain.
Searing . . .
Throbbing . . .
Pain.
And blood.
And home.
And pain.
And noise.
And Mary.
Train waiting . . .
Flame spurting . . .
Mary, home, dinner.

Mary? Dinner? Train? Waiting?
Only mud.
Cold . . .
Black . . .
Mud
And pain.

Married? Home? Job?
Job!
Can't use you . . .
Just taken . . .
All filled up . . .
Need a man . . . but
If you were white.
White?
If you were white?
White . . . black . . . blood . . .
Red!
With noise and mud and pain.

Hungry, job, white.
Army.
An even break.
Fight.
Democracy.
Freedom.
Job.
In the Army.
Can't understand

in the Army
men all Black,
officers all white
in the Army.

U.S.O. parties . . .
Hostesses white.
Whites danced
but Blacks
sat in corner
and watched.
Damn!
Blacks liked to dance
too.
Whites . . . danced.
Blacks . . . watched.
Good time with . . .
Mud . . . blood . . . pain.

No more pain . . .
No more blood . . .
No more mud . . . . . .
Just . . . stiff . . . numb . . .
Army.
Army! . . . came overseas.
Had a job to do,
the officer said,
and if we did it right
maybe . . .
after the war . . .

maybe . . .
there would be
equality, democracy
for all.

Came 5000 miles to fight for freedom.
Freedom for all.
Whether skin was White or Red or Brown or Yellow
. . . or Black.
Fight
to show
that there was something
to fight for.
And then . . . the charge . . .
And the rifles
that spurted flame . . . and noise . . .
and blood . . . and pain . . . and mud.

It was quiet now.
Everyone was gone.
No more wet
or cold.
Quiet . . . and peaceful . . .
And calm. . . and warm . . . and sleepy.
Up ahead,
past a sun yet to shine
golden sunbeams
opened wide
into a land
where there was
equality
and freedom.

WAR IS A WHORE

They say there are no atheists
in trenches or in foxholes.
They say there cannot be a God
to let men die like moles.

They say that soldiers must be brave,
not flinch in sight of death.
They teach you to protect yourself
to escape the enemy's wrath.

They say that life is sacred,
like a temple on a hill.
They tell you that your mission
is to shoot and kill.

They tell you that hypocrisy
is the language of a whore,
but when you are in combat
the real whore is the war.

A SOLDIER'S THOUGHTS

Just before the Battle of the Bulge (we called it "the breakthrough," the media gave it a more memorable name), there was an eerie quiet in that area of Belgium near the border of France. I recall standing guard duty one brisk but not cold night, just after a light rain, the stillness and freshness helping me almost forget for a few moments that I was in the middle of a war. I know that a lot of other soldiers, in the days preceding the German counterattack, must have felt the same way. It was early December, 1944, and prompted me, then 19 years old, to write the following poem.

It's the kind of night
when you can reach out and touch the sky,
when you can breathe the wet air and mist
and take a handful of dew and put it in your pocket.

It's the kind of night
when the air is cool and yet so warm,
when you can look up for a rainbow
but there is none—because it is night.

It's the kind of night
when the storm has washed away world's cares,
cleansed the world of its troubles
for a moment, seemingly so.

It's a night when streets are newly washed
and rooftops glisten in soft moonlight,
when stars twinkle a bit brighter
and life seems just a little finer.

It's a night when you want to hop into your car
and just ride, the tires eating mile after mile of dark glass,
when you want to walk endlessly and breathe in
big gulps of newborn freshness.

It's a night when you remember the trickling brook
reaching higher and flowing faster,
when winged insects were too wet to fly
and crickets sang in hoarse damp notes.

It's a night when you used to open the windows
and look at the bright and shiny streets,
when you used to step out on the porch
and gaze at the twinkling grasses.

It's a night
that brings back many memories,
that makes you want to do many deeds,
that takes your mind to many places.

It's the kind of night
when
more than anything else
you want to be home.

AN ENGLISH GIRL'S WWII LAMENT

In the summer of 1945, with the war in Europe over, I had a week's leave in London. While there were many American servicemen stationed in England during the war, those of us in combat on the continent didn't have the opportunity to socialize with the British. More specifically, with the women. On this first visit there, I saw the sometimes serious and sometimes frivolous relationships between American soldiers and British lasses, and wrote this poem. While not quite the "ugly American" of novelist Sinclair Lewis, some Americans who fancied themselves super-sophisticates or irresistible lotharios earned the good-natured and friendly satire of some British women.

Dear old England's not the same.
We dreaded invasion. Well, it came,
although it's not the beastly Hun,
the God-damned Yankee Army's come.

We see them on the tram and bus,
there isn't room for both of us.
We walk, to let them have our seats,
then get run over by their Jeeps.

They moan about our lukewarm beer,
claim beer's like water over here,
yet, after having two or more
they end up lying on the floor.

You should see them try to dance.
They grab a partner, start to prance.
When you're half-dead, they stop and smile,
ask, "How'd you like that, honeychile?"

We see them try to jitterbug,
they twist and turn and pull and hug.
It's enough to make a Buddhist jealous,
yet Yanks are civilized—so they tell us.

The officers give us cause to smile
with their superior habits and facades of guile.
We wonder if they're mice or men,
decide they're wolves and avoid their den.

With admiration we would stare
at all the ribbons these Yanks wear.
We think of deeds so brave and daring
that won the ribbons they are wearing.

Alas, many have not yet fought the Hun.
No glorious battles have they won.
those pretty ribbons just denote
they crossed the sea, just now, in boats.

To our British accents they all look hazy.
They think we're daft. We think they're crazy.
But to our Allies we must be nice.
They love us, just as cats love mice.

They laugh at us for drinking tea,
but a funnier sight you'll never see
than a gum-chewing Yank with a dumb-looking face.
He'd raise a laugh most anyplace.

They tell us they can shoot and fight.
It's true they fight when they are tight.
We must admit their shooting's fine
when they shoot us a ruddy come-on line.

They tell us we've got teeth like pearls,
they love our hair and the way it curls.
Our eyes would dim the brightest star,
we're competition for Hedy LaMarr.

We are their life, their love, their all
and for no other would they fall.
They'll love us, dear, till death do part.
If we should leave, we'll break their heart.

But then they leave us broken-hearted.
Their ship has sailed, our love departed.
We wait for mail, it never comes
and then we know that we've been dumb.

In a different town, in a different place,
To a different girl with a different face:
"I love you, honey, please be mine."
Same old Yank, same old line!

WORDSWORTH, WHERE ART THOU?

My early introduction to poetry included England's "romantic" poets. As a teenager, the designation itself was a special attraction for me. To my pleasant surprise, I found that those early nineteenth century bards had much more on their minds than just "romance." They unearthed the essence of the real world, of the hopes and failures of society. The first poem I remember memorizing was Wordsworth's "the world is too much with us; late and soon, getting and spending, we lay waste our powers; little we see in nature that is ours." Had any philosopher or political novelist put it so strong and clear? How true and vital today! In 1802 Wordsworth wrote a poem that called on the great poet Milton to figuratively return and bring manner, virtue, freedom and power to a stagnant and selfish England. In 2016 I wished Wordsworth could return and help change an America and world fallen into selfish, insensitive greed and power.

Wordsworth, thou should be with us this day.
The world, it seems, hath given its soul away.
The cries of those who suffer
as life turns colder and rougher
fall on ears that do not hear,
tuned to self-frivolity,
to vendors' cries
to wealth amassed,
to notions of superiority.
Wilt thou channel Milton once again?

Wordsworth, come back to us through mystic call,
lead us back to nature, one and all.
Free us from the pall that stifles our better natures
and leads our minds and hearts to icons and idols,
away from that in which true wisdom dwells.
We must look not for miracles in an empty sky,
ignoring the pleas of those who suffer and die.
The world, indeed, is too much with us
who kneel before an empty bower.
Help us stand, instead, before the human wave and flower.

FROM MY BEDROOM WINDOW

I saw Joe DiMaggio and Lou Gehrig play in Yankee Stadium. I saw Franklin Delano Roosevelt ride by in an open limousine. I saw Jackie Robinson steal home at Ebbets Field. I saw what discrimination, prejudice and hate engender as World War II in Europe ended and the pitiful remnants who survived the concentration camps struggled to continue to live. I shook hands with President Lyndon Johnson in the White House upon his signing of the Public Broadcasting Act of 1967. During the 1930s great depression I sat on Brooklyn park benches next to Civil War veterans whose last days were spent in abject poverty while entrepreneurs bought penthouses in Manhattan and villas in Palm Beach. I wish I had sat with the romantic poets in England's Lake District as they put quill pens to paper.

From my bedroom window
in the darkness of the night
I see a pool of blue-green water
rippling
under slowly falling raindrops
then roiling
under gusts of warm wind.

I peer into the blackness to
see more,
into the depths searching
for
I know not what,
hidden under the water's
movement.

I look for a reflection
of the moon
hovering o'er the sea,
piercing the black cloak covering
the water,
pulling my imagination into its ray
of light.

A mermaid shyly hiding from my sight?
A pleasure dome waiting for a prince,
a princess, or Kubla Kahn?
A Tintern Abbey's walls floating unfettered
by age or gravity?
Water lilies reaching out to a shore of
golden daffodils?

By the water's edge, poets with quill pens
dipping into wells of ink,
etching onto paper eternal words,
and to their pages of rhymes signing names like
Wordsworth, Shelley, Byron, Coleridge, Keats
and even
Shakespeare.

For a fleeting—too fleeting—a moment
I feel that I am among them,
but like a ghostly apparition I disappear
and see myself still in the darkness of the night
peering, searching
to see beneath the blue-green waters for that
which does not exist above its depths.

The wind subsides
and the raindrops cease
and the blue-green water
is tinged with the yellow and orange
of the sun
as night
gently gives way to day.

The water is stilled, my illusions
stilled with it.
No horizon at the water's edge,
no ships
with white sails,
no beach,
not even a grain of sand.

Only concrete blocks
comprise my night-time sea.
A distant thought,
an amorphous dream
as daylight wipes away
the décor
of my night-time visions?

But another night is coming
and in the darkness
of a storm,
imagined or not,
I will search again the dreams
within my blue-green sea
as I look out from my bedroom window.

TUMBLING

Tumbling through the treetops,
keep from crying aloud
as stars and sun are shimmering
o'er countries wearing a shroud.

Tumbling through a lifetime
part of an uncaring crowd,
seeing leaves and lives a'wither
from high above the ground.

Blind to what's below,
feeling vain and proud
above the fields and forests,
ignoring heads deep-bowed.

Men, women and children
are awfully hard to see,
and seeing them is really hard
when the priority is ME.

THE DEER

It's a far cry from the pastoral quiet of the English Lake District to the hustle-bustle of a big-city center, whether a five-hour drive to London or a three-thousand mile flight to New York City. We have all seen the iconic films of crowds of people hustling into subways like cattle on their way to penned-in office cubicles, eagerly awaiting the time to return to the subways away from the sheafs of paper covering wooden desks. We wonder whether they daydream of escaping, running free through forests and streams. The world is still too much with us.

As the deer runs through the forest
seeking the quenching waters
of the leaf-covered stream,
we run over hot concrete
seeking the quenching taste
of mercantile green.

The deer runs free from stream to stream
as we sit fixed, only daring to dream
of forests and glens, our real world
not even wondering if or when
the dream will or can replace
the suffocating fen.

Do we mock those who dare to touch
our feared but wanted sight?
Unknown others, why should they be free
to breathe deeply of unpolluted air
and not share
our own polluted plight?

Nodding across wooden mantles
holding endless paper sheafs,
watching for the witching hour,
the signal of prescribed relief,
moving from one darkness to another,
from upright to pillowed sleep.

Light fades, but restless sleep
brings no forests or waters deep,
but piercing blackness
pricking the ache within.
Shall we acknowledge?
Dare we seek?
For a fleeting moment
eyes close, to follow the deer's soft steps,
to follow the rocky trail
toward the healing freedom,
the impossible dream
of the leaf-covered stream.

For a moment, too brief a moment
we stand at the edge of a shimmering sea,
or is it Morpheus calling me and thee?
But look:
no concrete, no paper sheafs
drowning the sought-for dream.

Daylight shatters the curtain,
the deer departs, no forest or glen,
no leaf-covered stream.
Can we acknowledge the grief
that marks the concrete ribbons,
the wooden mantles with paper sheafs?

SLEEP

Blessed sleep,
Why have you deserted me?
Have I transgressed
against your shadowed healing?

What artificial light pierces
the dark warmth of your embrace,
to roil my brain,
to untimely stir its state of rest?

O, shut the magic door.
It is not yet morn,
not yet time
for thought or sound or sight.

Shut out the intruder,
bury it in my psyche,
push it to the corners of my senses,
send it into temporary oblivion.

Too late. Too late.
Consciousness has spoken.
Words unsaid but thought
Have broken the spell of Morpheus.

The mind has stirred the body.
The pillow soft
is now a rocky ledge
unable to quell the awakened senses.

A sheet and a blanket,
protection against outside elements,
are no bulwark against
one's own inner self.

Awake! Awake! The unwanted words
beget even less wanted feelings.
The bed is suddenly a stranger,
evicting a yawning, tired, glazed-eyed body.

O, bed and pillow, take me back,
let me disappear again,
even for a short while,
into the solitude of silence.

But it is not to be.
Devoutly wished, a plea unheard.
The paradise of sleep
has closed its portals.

To pace the floor?
It makes the pulse beat faster.
To sit and read?
It makes the mind a sharper master.

What is left
but to cogitate and write
and make the night
a complete disaster!

SAVE A TEARDROP

Save a little teardrop,
put it on a shelf,
take it down and use it
when feeling sorry for yourself.

Save a little pity
for a day that's blue.
Use it for the people
who need it more than you.

Save some understanding
when the world looks grey
for those you disagree with.
It's no longer yesterday.

O' AMERICA, NOVEMBER 8, 2016

Part I:

Lilac no longer blooms
in courtyard or garden
or glen.

The statue
that lights the way to liberty
stands dark and mute.

O, America, where has your promise gone?
America, what fate has thrust you
into the belly of the beast?

Orange groves in Florida turn to ice.
Apples fall blighted from Washington trees.
Grapes of California die on the vine.

Ivy, green with expectation
shielding our eyes from ugliness,
turns brown and withers.

Yellow stalks of corn
are now stained with the
color of hate.

O, land that held promise for so many,
open arms that filled prairie and city,
forests of freedom that stretched from sea to sea.

O, land that once welcomed all
yearning to breathe free,
where have you gone?

O, city and town and village
that made impossible dreams possible,
where have you gone?

Land meant for tranquility and peace
overcome by sheets of white once more,
not snows of winter, but of hate and terror.

The promise of majority rule is drowned,
suffocated in a system
made for king-makers.

Of thee I mourn, baby,
summer, autumn, winter,
you're forlorn, baby.

There's no silver lining
in the sky above
just the sounds of Twitter substituting for love.

The songs are gone, giving way to grief,
tongues are silent now,
heard only in restive sleep.

Weep for your country, cry for your land.
Will tears wash away the blight of bigotry?
Will sighs blow away the stench of poverty?

How many uplifted arms
will dare halt the hands
that now rock the cradle?

Willows weep with sorrow,
owls screech with anger,
mountains shake with fear.

The people cry,
O, country once betrothed to us,
where are you now?

How long to restore
our country's soul,
our land, our seas, our sky?

Lilac no longer blooms
in courtyard, garden, or glen.
When will it again?

Part II:

Do not despair,
no longer weep.
The lilac roots are deep.
They froze at Valley Forge
and rose at Appomattox,
trampled by Pinkertons,
rescued by daughters and sons
who marched for liberty
from farm and village and city
to hold high the promise of America.

Hear the sounds of freedom,
footsteps on the freedom road,
every step a roar
louder than before.
Raise our voices now,
dispel the gloom,
for our right to speak and assemble
and protest those who would dissemble
and try to halt the
lilacs bloom.

Don't let our voices go for naught,
make lilacs bloom
in every courtyard, every street,
in every vision, in every deed
for every person
in every thought.

SILENCE

Fear not the tyrant's breath,
the fork'd tongue not yet
stirring that which doth beget
the souls of youth to rise and set
the course that leads to freedom met.

Nay, truth cowers in hidden corners
of the tyrant's reign, its mourners
hiding, too, letting perfidy have its way,
infamy holding sway,
alternative facts the doctrine of the day.

Timid souls, afraid to dig their heels
and shout nay to those who steal
the heart and mind of what is good and real,
the conscience of our commonweal,
the song that lets our freedoms peal.

Shall you, shall I, shall we stay mute
while evil tongues destroy the truth
and turn to dust hope and promise grand?
Or shall we rise at last to raise our hand
and take back our dear and cherished land?

THERE CAME A TYRANT

One of the books analyzing the genesis of the 1930s-1940s Holocaust visited upon the world by Germany and its supporters is entitled Hitler's Willing Executioners. *Tyrants cannot gain power without the consent—or apathy—of the public. Wordsworth's 1807 poem, "Thought of a Briton on the Subjugation of Switzerland" is germane to many countries.*

There came a tyrant to my native land.
Alas, my friends and neighbors
lent a hand and put him into power.
Solons, once free and proud, did kneel and cower.

No, Wordsworth, that tyrant's not for the Swiss
although one might inadvertently wish
he would impose on some other nation's realm
and that sanity would take lead of our helm.

How long would kith and kin yield to this yoke,
a tyrant seen by the world as a joke,
but whose imposition upon our weal
is far from humorous, is all too real?

Will we yield of our vaunted liberty,
cede our moral mien, our integrity,
or shall we, feet to the ground, take a stand
and drive far from us the tyrant's cruel brand?

Or shall we hide, this day, minute, and hour,
self-banished, one and all, to our ivory tower?
Where hath gone the bravery and the pride
that drove former tyrants well from our side?

Are we now, and will be, dead from numbing fear,
abandoning the freedoms we hold dear?
Or shall we, as before, to solution
in the spirit of '76, a new revolution?

RIP: A SIXTY-YEAR LAMENT

A rite of passage for many of us growing up in Brooklyn, New York, in the 1930s was to become Brooklyn Dodger fans. Our psyches rose and fell commensurate with the fortunes of our Ebbets Field baseball team. For many years we spent the baseball seasons largely in gloom as the Dodgers' mantra perennially seemed to be "wait until next year!" Next year finally came in the 1950s when the Dodgers won four National League pennants and, in 1955, the only World Series won by the Brooklyn team. It was a new era for Dodger fans. However, in 1957 the owners of the team saw huge dollar signs in the hills of Los Angeles and moved the Dodgers to the west coast, leaving Brooklyn's baseball fans bereft.

They're gone.
Pete, Pee-wee and Jackie
entertaining the
knothole gang
by crashing into walls,
hustling infield rollers.,
and stealing home with a bang.

They're gone.
Dolph and Cookie and Leo.
No lip to the umps.
No soda or peanuts or crackerjacks.
No cries from the
twenty-five cent bleacher seats,
"Wait until next year!"
No more we'll be chumps.

And Hoyt ain't hoit anymore.

They're gone.
Van Lingle the Mungo and Sandy the K
and Campy, Newk and Preacher,
and Mickey, who dropped the third strike,
kicking the game away.

Even after Ralph hurled
the shot heard round the world
we were soothed by the guy in the catbird seat.
Red's voice helped take away the heat.

There was sweet-swinging Duke
And Gil's four in a game.
Why aren't they
in baseball's hall of fame?

We can still boo the Giants,
But it just ain't the same.

Waiting year after year
for a moment delirious,
to root for the trolley boys,
at last, in 1955, as they win
the Woild Serious.

Finally, some fame,
more games to be won,
big houses to talley,
and the money ain't lame.
But poof, they were gone.
A pox on O'Malley.

A pseudo-team now in L.A.
copping a cherished name.
A usurper.
A pretender.
A thief.
For shame! For shame!

It's gone.
They're gone.
Rest in Peace, Ebbets Field.
Rest in Peace, Brooklyn Dodgers.

CYBERSPACE

As I sit with my body bent,
straining to see the screen before me.,
my neck feels torn and rent.
I am not computer meant,
to pick and click for eternity.

The icons loom too large for some,
but are miniscule to me.
I find they're hard to overcome
and often now lose my aplomb
over Control and Z and Alt and V.

Shall I take a step that some think bold
and move away from pen and ink,
pretend that I am six years old
and face whatever may unfold
as I bravely go from link to link?

If cyberspace is here to stay,
I'll pretend this is no longer me
and let computers have their way,
with Facebook, Twitter and Linked-in okay
as I cede cyberspace its victory.

MARLOWE ON A SOCCER FIELD

The foot falls heavy on the ball
where lightness is required.
The legs are stiff, the knees both ache.
The body full is tired.

Strive to catch a second breath,
the game has only started.
Almost ninety minutes more,
a role not for faint-hearted.

Once more a run up o'er the field
and quickly then a run back,
to breathe and gasp, and gasp and breathe
to join the mass attack.

A header here, a long kick there,
ten others in the fray.
Pass quickly to the one in front,
keep the ball in play.

Half-time yet? You wish too quick,
the clock too slowly rolls.
Breathe more deeply, retie your shoes,
try again to reach that goal.

Back and forth, forth and back,
the field seems larger now.
Stop that kick, intercept that pass,
with sweat upon your brow.

A second wind, new strength it brings,
avoid the yellow card.
Hurrah, a goal, the game is won.
That didn't seem too hard.

FEAR

So many of us say we love animals. Yet, so many of us take pleasure in killing them. I recall a cartoon showing a little girl with her arm around a pet calf. The caption read: "man is the only animal who eats other animals he makes friends with."

I hide my face
and try to find a place
to burrow deep
and hope my life to keep
as those with guns
fire fast and free
and shoot to kill . . . me.

I'm only an animal, of course,
and they do have remorse
if perchance they hit and take
one of their own lives by mistake.
Not so for us.
Yet, we have feelings, too,
whether in the wild or in a zoo.

Yes, we have kith and kin
that we hold dear within,
and cry when men in red draw near;
we shake and quiver in fear.
Will they kill us just for sport?
And when the hunt at last is done
were we shot dead just for fun?

LIFE SPAN

Perceptions of life and age change as age and life change. In 1947, at age 22, I wrote the first part of this poem; in 2017, at 92, the second.

The life of man spans eighty years
in three parts divided, to pause
in unequal number
and for different cause.

The babe, the youth, the man
count twenty that move too slow
with impatient look to the future,
to prick and goad the present to go.

From twenty to sixty the future has sped
in present struggle, security to beget
as husband, father, family king,
passions dedicated, energies set.

Sans hope, sans years, sans life
the final twenty toll requiem fast.
Neither present nor future remain
as thoughts turn to life in the past.

       * * *

Now that I'm ninety years and more
it's time to think and revise the score.
With so much to do, so much unsaid,
one looks to countless years ahead.
Whether ten or twenty or only one
life will be full until I'm done.

AM I MY GRANDFATHER?

Am I my grandfather
who I never knew,
when I look in the mirror
and from the ages view
a face whose very look
is on an old photo in a family book?

Each time I look, I hope to see
some visage stately and sublime,
but try as I might
I can only find
a face that is simply
his and mine.

THE SUN

In the early 1980s, before the Berlin wall came down, I visited East and West Berlin. In the west sector I met a museum artist and photographer, Dieter Kramer, one of whose display photos was of a deteriorating, ugly, dirty, dismal section of slum buildings where Turkish immigrant workers in West Berlin were forced to live. This was in ironic contrast to the new, airy, clean apartment houses I had seen for similar low-income workers in much poorer East Berlin. The caption, in German, on Kramer's West Berlin photo—a framed signed copy of which I have in my home—reads: "Every day the sun comes up . . . but not over everywhere."

Light up the sky
morning sun
golden ball
shimmering high.

Send your bright rays
over land and sea,
mountains and valleys,
announcing the day.

Wake up the farms,
claxon the cities,
for those still abed
sound the alarm.

Warm up our hearts,
glisten our faces,
without your embrace
the day never starts.

O, gift so sublime,
don't wander or wane,
stay with us forever
. . . or at least half the time.

KITTY DITTY

Perchance have you seen
a pussycat green
that rambled the streets of the town?

Dressed up for a lark
and a stroll in the park
in a pink and white shimmering gown?

What say you there, cat?
said a man in a hat,
his face in a terrible frown.

I say to you, sir,
said the cat with a purr,
why wear you the face of a clown?

It troubles me, cat,
and I won't stop to chat,
that a feline seems clad for a crown.

Why think you that I
(not batting an eye)
am not fit for a life of renown?

And with a flick of her tail
she eluded that male
and went on her merry-go-round.

THE SOUL IS NOT BETRAYED

In 1946, back in college after World War II, I found courses in philosophy especially stimulating. Like many 21-year-olds I sought answers to who I was, who we were, and what our relationship and responsibility to life were. I wrote the following poem at that time.

The cup of gold calls from the west
but sensual joy delays the quest.
The plush puts strong will to the test.
The soul is not betrayed.

Through work and toil, through sweat and tears
the goal is foremost, temptation dear,
faith unquestioned in another sphere.
The soul is not betrayed.

On wings of steel and silent tread
to bleak unknown the five have sped.
Though no sign, neither hope nor dread,
the soul is not betrayed.

WERE I TO CLIMB EVERY HILL, 2017

Were I to climb every hill in Christendom
seeking answers to thoughts that leave me numb,
not knowing what is true and what is false,
would I be dancing an unending waltz?

Were I to pore over every line in an ancient Torah,
seeking refuge from unrepentant horror,
my mind filled with fact, not fantasy,
would I still be bound in apostasy?

If I recited all the Qur'an verses,
hoping to glean a glimmer of life's purpose,
would I know more than other beliefs
or feel stranded on endless reefs?

If I learned to chant a Buddhist mantra,
seeking refuge in Dharma or Sangha,
to meditate with calm and insight,
would that make my life alright?

Or should I turn to flower and tree,
to billowing wave and shimmering sea,
to mountain top and sparkling plain,
or is all seeking just in vain?

LIFE IS

Life is a music box,
an organ-grinder's playground,
a symphony orchestra,
Alexander's ragtime band.

Life is a pas-de-deux,
a tutu on tip-toes,
a rhumba, tango, shimmy-and-shake,
a waltz, the twist, jitterbug and Charleston.

Life is a play,
sometimes a drama,
sometimes a comedy,
sometimes a farce.

Life is a painting,
often surreal,
often abstract,
a Mona Lisa and a can of soup.

Life is a book,
open and closed,
non-fiction to think,
fiction to dream.

Life is a poem,
be it short, be it long.
You write the stanzas,
you choose the rhymes.

DREAMS
If we did not have dreams, would we have philosophers and scientists? If we did not have dreams, would there be new worlds to explore? If we did not have dreams, would we care about better tomorrows? If we did not have dreams, would there be poets?

If you close your eyes
even on a cloudy night
you can see
a sky full of stars,
much brighter
although much further away
than the reflection
of Mars.

Other than in movies,
where you can travel
to the stars and Mars
on a whim
they remain
beyond our reach,
beyond the limits
of our outer rim.

If our reach remains
beyond our means
we need to only
enhance our dreams
and imagine we are on
a distant plain,
free from dust or heat
or cold or rain.

Our deep desires,
bold and bright,
shining icons
of sound and light
endless gardens
and pleasure domes,
from whose embrace
never to roam.

To live, to love
in that distant place,
forever grand,
forever more.
After all,
isn't that
what
dreams are for?

www.ingramcontent.com/pod-product-compliance
Lightning Source LLC
LaVergne TN
LVHW091319080426
835510LV00007B/561